The ABCs
of Royalty

by Jaclyn Jaycox

illustrated by Gustavo Eriza

raintree

a Capstone company — publishers for children

A is for (happily ever) after.

A witch's spell is broken. The prince and princess fall in love and get married. In most fairy tales, there is a happily ever after.

B is for ball.

The princess arrives at the ball wearing her loveliest dress. The prince asks her to dance. As the music plays, they twirl around the dance floor.

C is for castle.

Princesses live in castles overlooking the kingdom. Big castles have hundreds of rooms! Outside, they have gardens full of beautiful flowers.

4

 **is for daughter.**

A princess is the daughter of a king and queen. They will teach her how to be a good princess. She might become queen some day and rule the kingdom.

E is for enchanted.

A witch has put a spell on the prince and turned him into a frog! Only a kiss from a princess can turn the enchanted frog back into a prince.

F is for fairy godmother.

In fairy tales, a fairy godmother has magical powers. She can turn pumpkins into carriages and rags into ballgowns. She can make the princess's dreams come true!

G is for gown.

A princess's wardrobe is full of beautiful gowns. Some might be pink with sashes of white. Others may be blue with sequins so bright!

H is for handsome prince.

A handsome prince must also be very brave.
He must tame the dragon guarding the castle
to save the princess!

I is for imagination.

What would it be like to be a princess and live in a castle? Go to royal balls and wear tiaras? Just close your eyes and use your imagination!

J is for jewellery.

Princesses wear beautiful bracelets, sparkling necklaces and glittery gems. They wear their best jewellery on special occasions.

K is for kingdom.

A kingdom is a country ruled by a king and queen.
They make important decisions and look after the people.

12

L is for lady-in-waiting.

A lady-in-waiting helps the princess dress and keeps her schedule. The lady-in-waiting is also the princess's friend.

M is for magic.

Fairy tales are full of magic. A magic wand turns Cinderella into a princess for one night. A poisonous apple puts Snow White into a deep sleep.

N is for noble.

Nobles are people who are born royal.
A princess and her family are all nobles.

O is for once upon a time.

Fairy tales usually start with "Once upon a time". These magical stories tell tales of gentle princesses, wicked witches, fire-breathing dragons and brave princes.

16

P is for princess.

There are real-life princesses all around the world. Saudi Arabia, Sweden and the United Kingdom all have princesses and royal families.

 **is for queen.**

A queen is sometimes married to a king. Her children are princes and princesses. She is wise and brave, and she teaches her children how to be royal.

 **is for royal.**

Just like the king, queen and prince, a princess is part of the royal family. She may be in line to take over the throne.

19

S is for sparkles.

Diamonds twinkle. Glass slippers shine. Jewellery gleams. When a princess is all dressed up, she sparkles from head to toe!

T is for tiara.

A tiara is a crown that princesses wear for special occasions. Tiaras are covered in glittery diamonds and colourful jewels.

U is for unite.

As part of the royal family, a princess must help to unite the kingdom. She goes to events and celebrations to bring people together.

V is for Virtue.

A princess is respected for her virtue.
She must always do what is right.

W is for wand.

Witches and fairies use wands to cast magical spells. Magic can be good or bad. A bad fairy put a spell on Sleeping Beauty. The princess pricked her finger on a spindle and fell asleep.

X is for eXample.

Princesses are a very good example to follow. They are kind and caring, and they spend time helping people.

25

Y is for Your Royal Highness.

When meeting a princess, address her as "Your Royal Highness".
Don't forget to bow or curtsy!

Z is for dazzle.

The royal family's crown jewels are dazzling.
The crown jewels are worn for special events.
They are passed down from parents to children.

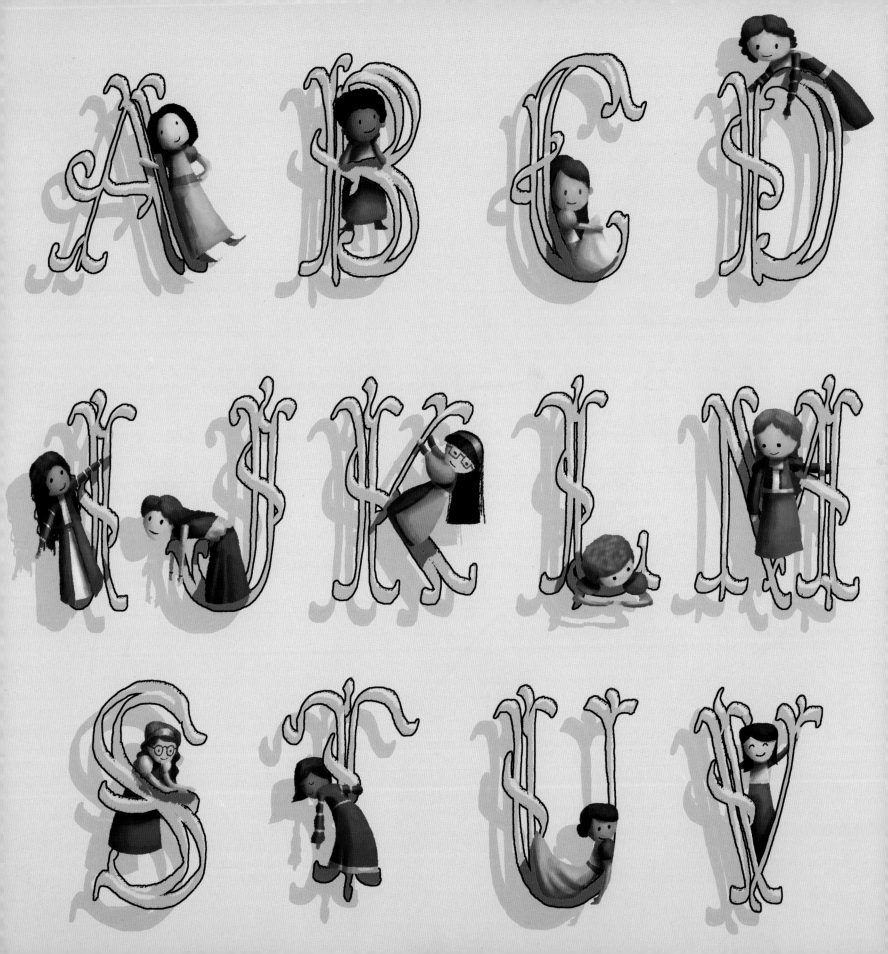

Glossary

ball fancy party where people get dressed up and dance

carriage vehicle with wheels, sometimes pulled by horses

crown jewels the crown, sceptre and other items covered in gold or jewels that are used by a member of a royal family during formal events

enchanted put under a magic spell

fairy tale simple magical story

gown dress

kingdom country that has a king or queen as its ruler

noble person of high rank or birth

occasion special or important event

unite to be together as one

Read More

Cinderella (Fairy Tales), Ed Bryan (Nosy Crow, 2015)

I Want a Bedtime Story! (Little Princess), Tony Ross
(Andersen Press, 2016)

Princes and Princesses (Royalty), Sally Lee
(Pebble Plus, 2013)

Websites

www.princess.disney.co.uk/
Explore the world of Disney princesses with games and
creative activities.

www.theveryfairyprincess.com/princesses.html
Read about real princesses around the world.

Index

Raintree is an imprint of Capstone Global Library Limited, a company incorporated in England and Wales having its registered office at 264 Banbury Road, Oxford, OX2 7DY – Registered company number: 6695582

www.raintree.co.uk
myorders@raintree.co.uk

Text © Capstone Global Library Limited 2017
The moral rights of the proprietor have been asserted.

Editor: Gillia Olson
Designer: Ashlee Suker
Art Director: Nathan Gassman
Production Specialist: Katy LaVigne
The illustrations in this book were created digitally.

ISBN 978 1 4747 2443 2
20 19 18 17 16
10 9 8 7 6 5 4 3 2 1

British Library Cataloguing in Publication Data
A full catalogue record for this book is available from the British Library.

Every effort has been made to contact copyright holders of material reproduced in this book. Any omissions will be rectified in subsequent printings if notice is given to the publisher.

All the Internet addresses (URLs) given in this book were valid at the time of going to press. However, due to the dynamic nature of the Internet, some addresses may have changed, or sites may have changed or ceased to exist since publication. While the author and publisher regret any inconvenience this may cause readers, no responsibility for any such changes can be accepted by either the author or the publisher.

Printed and Bound in China.

Other Titles in this Series

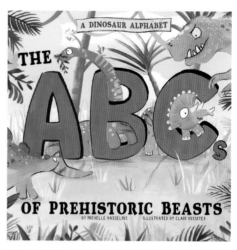